Rice

Marianne Morrison

Contents

A Popular Food

More people eat rice than any other food. It is nutritious, which means it is good for you. It gives you energy and fills you up. Rice is also very cheap and plentiful.

▲ A bowl of rice makes up a large part of the meal in many Asian countries.

In Asia, people usually eat rice two or three times a day. Rice is often a large part of a meal. In some Asian languages, the word for rice and the word for food are the same word. For example, in Chinese, the word for food and rice is *fan*. In other Asian languages, the same word means "eat" and "eat rice."

How Rice Began

There are many stories about rice and when it was first planted. Here is one tale from China.

Long ago in China, there were floods. When the floods ended, the people came down from the mountain. The floods had destroyed all their plants. There was no food. A dog suddenly appeared. He brought yellow seeds. The people planted the seeds. Rice grew, and the people were never hungry again.

Around the world, people eat rice in many dishes. They eat rice in soups, salads, and desserts. Other foods are made from rice. It is used to make foods such as noodles, flour, cereals, and snack foods.

rice vinegar

rice noodles

rice cakes

rice cereal

rice chips

rice snacks ▶

Growing Rice

No one really knows for sure when people began to grow rice. Some scientists believe people in India began growing rice for food over 6,000 years ago. Today, farmers all over the world grow rice. Rice is the number one food crop grown in the world.

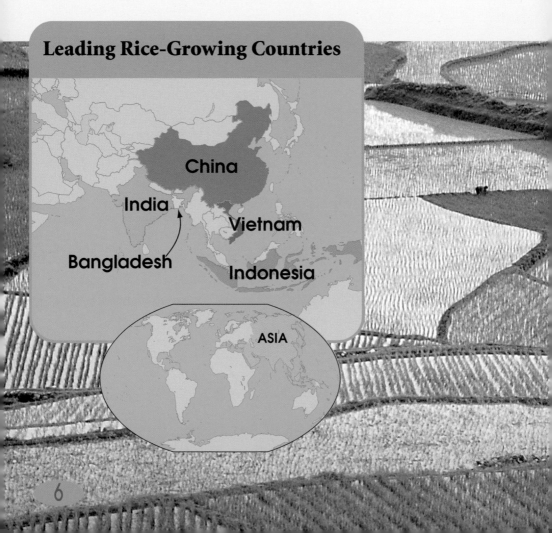

Leading Rice-Growing Countries

China

India

Vietnam

Bangladesh

Indonesia

ASIA

Rice grows best in areas that are wet and warm. During the growing season, temperatures should be at least 70° F (20° C). Rice grows best on lowlands, like river valleys, that can be easily flooded. But rice can also grow on higher lands that get steady rain.

▼ Rice grows in flooded fields in the lowlands of China.

The Rice Plant

Rice is a cereal grain like wheat, corn, and oats. The rice plant is a tall plant. It grows from 3 to 6 feet (1 to 2 meters) tall. At the end of each stem is a **head**. This head holds the **kernels** of rice. Each head holds from 60 to 150 kernels of rice.

Each kernel has a hard covering, called a **hull**, that is not good to eat. Inside each kernel are layers of bran and the rice grain, which is the part of the plant that we eat.

head

leaves

stems ▶

◀ roots

▼ Kernels of rice hang from the heads of a rice plant.

Farmers grow many different kinds of rice. Most people think of rice as white. But it can also be red, blue, purple, and even striped!

There are three basic kinds of rice. There are long, medium, and short grains. The grains differ in size and shape and how sticky they get when cooked. Long grain rice is thin. When cooked, the grains separate and the rice is dry and fluffy. Short and medium grains are fatter than long grains. When cooked, these grains stick together.

long grain

short grain

medium grain

Rice Farming

Farmers in most of Asia grow rice almost the same way that farmers did thousands of years ago. Most of the work is done by women and most of it is done by hand. Every **seedling** is planted in the mud by hand. Some farmers use wooden plows pulled by water buffaloes.

Rice grows best in shallow water. Farmers plant seedlings in flat fields called **paddies**. Paddy fields have low dirt walls all around them. These fields are filled with water. Gates are opened to let the water in and out.

Some farmers in Asia grow rice on hills. They cut into the hills to make **terraces**, or large steps. The water flows down the terraces and keeps the rice plants wet.

◄ This farmer in China plows a field with a water buffalo.

Rice grows in terraced fields cut into the side of a hill in Indonesia. ▶

In some countries such as Japan, Italy, and the United States, farmers use machines to plant rice. They plant rice in early spring. They plant on level land where there is a good supply of water. They plant in areas where the temperatures are warm during the growing season.

Farmers use a machine pulled by a tractor to seed their fields. Some rice fields are so large that farmers use planes to seed their fields. The seeds planted by plane are soaked with water first. The soaking makes the seeds heavy enough to sink when dropped. The plane passes over the field, dropping the seeds.

▼ Rice grows in a field in the United States.

12

Once the rice plants begin to grow, the field is flooded with water. Farmers build solid dirt walls called **levees** to hold in the water. They divide their fields into small ponds. The ponds work like paddies. Water flows in and out of the rice fields through gates. By the middle of summer, the dark, muddy fields are a bright, green carpet.

A plane drops seeds ▶ on a rice field.

Harvesting Rice

The rice fields have turned from bright green to golden yellow. It is time to **harvest**, or bring in, the rice. The rice plants are ripe.

In many Asian countries, farmers harvest the rice the same way it was done thousands of years ago. First, they drain the rice paddies. The water flows out. It takes two weeks for the land to dry.

Then, farmers harvest the rice by hand. They use a curved tool, called a sickle, to cut the stems. They tie the stems together and let them dry. The dried stems become straw.

The dried plant is ready for **threshing**. Farmers separate the kernels of grain from the rest of the plant. Then they remove the hulls. Finally, the farmers have the grain.

Almost all of the rice plant can be used for something. The straw is used to weave baskets, hats, and sandals and to make roofs. The hulls are used to make fertilizer.

A farmer uses a sickle to harvest rice in India.

▼ Workers thresh rice in Vietnam.

In some countries, farmers use machines to harvest and thresh the rice. The machine is called a **combine** because it does several steps at once, or combines steps.

First, the combine cuts the rice stems. It also gathers them in and plucks off the kernels. The damp rice is loaded on a truck and taken to a dryer. There, the rice is dried by heated air.

In some countries, the dried rice is taken to **mills**. A mill is a building that has machinery for grinding grain. In the mill, machines scrape the hull from the kernels to make brown rice. Machines take off the hull and the bran layers to make white rice.

▼ Farmers in the United States use combines to harvest their rice.

Selling Rice

Most rice is eaten in the countries where it is grown. However, some rice is traded. Some countries in Asia **export**, or sell rice to other countries. Thailand and Vietnam are the biggest exporters of rice.

▼ Rice is sold at outdoor markets in Vietnam.

The United States exports some of its rice. It also **imports** rice. That means it buys rice from other countries. It buys jasmine rice from Thailand and basmati rice from India and Pakistan.

Bags of rice are loaded onto a ship in the United States.

S.W.L. 25 M.T.   PORT OF SACRAMENTO

Rice Dishes

Rice dishes that used to be eaten in just a few countries are now eaten around the world. Here are some popular rice dishes. Which ones have you tried?

▼ Paella with yellow rice comes from Spain.

Sushi is a Japanese dish ▶ made with seaweed.

◀ Rice pudding is a popular dessert in Great Britain.

Jambalaya is a common meal in the southern parts of the United States. ▶

Next time you eat rice, think about where it has come from. People eat rice in many different dishes and at many different times. Rice feeds the world!

Glossary

combine   machine used to harvest and thresh rice

export   to sell goods to another country

harvest   to gather or bring in a crop when it is ripe

head   the top part of the rice plant that holds the kernels of rice

hull   the hard covering around a grain of rice

import   to buy goods from another country

kernel   individual grain of rice

levee   walls made of dirt used to hold water in an area

mill   factory where grain is ground into flour or meal

paddy   field in which rice is grown

seedling   young plant grown from a seed

terrace   one of a series of flat areas cut into the side of a hill like steps

thresh   to separate the kernels of grain from the plant on which it is grown

Index